TELL ME ABOUT WRITERS AND ILLUSTRATORS

QUENTIN BLAKE

written by
Chris Powling

Evans
Evans Brothers Limited

Published by Evans Brothers Limited
2A Portman Mansions
Chiltern Street
London W1U 6NR

First published 1999
Reprinted 2001

Printed by Graficas Reunidas SA, Spain

British Library Cataloguing in Publication data.

Powling, Chris
Quentin Blake. - (Tell me about artists)
1. Blake, Quentin - Juvenile literature 2. Illustrators - Great Britain - Biography - Juvenile literature
I. Title
741.6'42'092

ISBN 0237519712

Acknowledgements

All photographs by Richard Newton except the photo on page 10 which is by Linda Kitson

Have you seen these pictures before?

Yes, it's Mister Magnolia, The BFG and a strange, wonderful creature called Zagazoo.

They were drawn by Quentin Blake. All over the world, children recognise his pictures at once. They're so full of life. But who is Quentin Blake? And how did he become one of the most famous illustrators alive? This book tells his story.

Quentin Blake hard at work on a new book.

Quentin grew up in Sidcup, Kent and went to Lamorbey Primary School. Later, he went to Chislehurst and Sidcup Grammar School. 'My childhood was very ordinary and very happy,' says Quentin. 'Except, of course, there was a war on.'

This was the Second World War.

Quentin when he was at primary school.

The school magazine in which Quentin published his first drawings.

Quentin's family wasn't at all artistic. 'My father worked in an office,' he says. 'And my mother looked after the house. In a way I was an only child - because my brother Ken was eleven years older than me.'

This meant he had plenty of time to himself.

Quentin and his parents at the seaside. Later, he owned two houses of his own by the sea.

He spent a lot of this time reading. And he drew, drew and drew. 'For hours on end I had a pencil in my hand,' Quentin laughs. 'Drawing was always what I loved best!'

Some of Quentin's first drawings and cartoons...

At grammar school, two teachers noticed how good he was. One was his Art teacher, Stanley Simmons. The other was his Latin teacher, Mrs Jackson. She showed Quentin's drawings to her husband, Alfred, who was a cartoonist on a famous magazine called 'Punch'. Quentin began sending 'Punch' his own cartoons. 'At first they came back with a note saying "Not quite". Then, suddenly, I got a cheque for seven guineas!'

He had sold his first drawing.

... and the magazine which first published him.

Quentin drawing at the Royal College of Art... a much bigger picture than usual.

Quentin went to Cambridge University to study English. Then he taught at the Royal College of Art.

His first children's book, called 'A Drink of Water', was written for him by his friend John Yeoman. After a while Quentin decided that he would like to illustrate a picture book, so he wrote one for himself. It was called 'Patrick'.

In 1980, another of his picture books, called 'Mister Magnolia', won the Kate Greenaway Medal.

'The best thing about it,' says Quentin, 'is that it tells you that a lot of people must like your books.'

He has won many more prizes since.

Perhaps Quentin's most famous book...

... and the children who tried to do it better!

By now Quentin was working with some very famous children's writers. 'This was a stroke of luck, really. Who wouldn't want to draw pictures for books by Joan Aiken, Russell Hoban, Michael Rosen and Roald Dahl?'

Quentin with Roald and Felicity Dahl.

Quentin working on a book with Michael Rosen.

Here Quentin is showing some French school children how he works... and is being filmed at the same time.

Of course, success brings problems of its own. There were letters from readers to answer. And trips to publishers to talk over new books. Invitations also arrived to appear on television or to visit schools, libraries and book fairs.

At home in London, where Quentin has lived for almost thirty years.

It hasn't always been easy for Quentin to fit everything in - especially when he became Head of Illustration at the Royal College of Art, in London.

He likes to escape to the seaside. He now has a house in Sussex, and another near Bordeaux, in France. 'These are my hideaways,' Quentin smiles. 'I go there to concentrate on drawing.'

The seaside is a favourite place for Quentin.

So how does Quentin start a new book? 'It all depends,' he says. 'Have I written the text or has someone else? And what kind of book is it? If it's a picture book, I'll need to plan it very carefully. Probably, I'll do some quick rough sketches first - just to show the ideas I have in mind.'

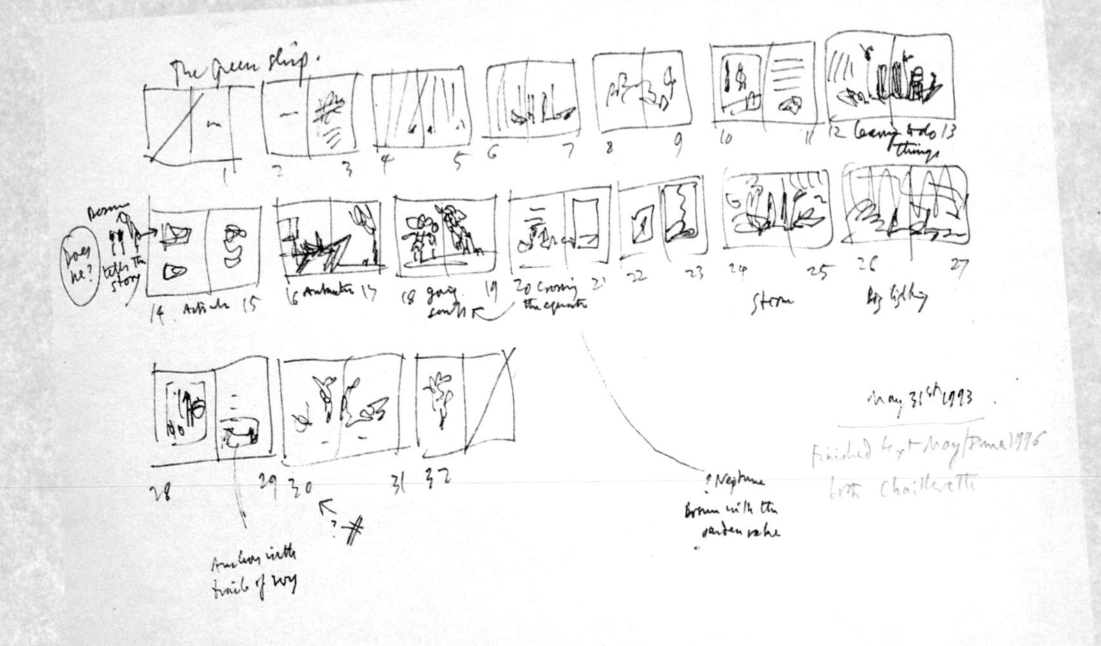

The start of a book by Quentin Blake... a quick, lively lay-out to help plan the story.

Here's how he organises a 'drawing day':

8.00 am. Get up. Wash, dress, have breakfast. Already I'm getting ready to draw. I try to relax - to quieten myself down yet stay wide awake.

9.00 am. Now, I'm warming up. I choose the right nib or pencil. I make sure that I have lots of paper ready of the right kind and the right size. In a way, I'm nervous. But I must begin sooner or later.

All his life, Quentin has loved drawing best of all.

9.30 am - 1.00 pm. With luck, I'm soon hard at work. Do I know already how the picture will look? Or am I making it up as I go along? It's a bit of both, really. Sometimes, the pen itself seems in charge! I need to keep my mind on the job, though - even if the phone or doorbell rings.

1.00 - 2.00 pm. Lunchtime. I may go out for a sandwich or to buy a newspaper. But what I must do is hold on to working 'mood'.

These days, Quentin has help in his office...

... so he can spend more time drawing.

Quentin, the light-box and a nearly finished drawing.

2.00 - 6.00 pm. I carry on drawing. I draw quickly, but I also spend a lot of time looking at what I have drawn and thinking about it. Sometimes, I use a light-box. This shines through an earlier drawing so I can do a fresh one on top. It helps me make changes but still keep what I really like.

For Quentin this would be a perfect day.

Quentin has illustrated more than 200 books altogether. Have you come across ‘Cockatoos’, ‘The Story of the Dancing Frog’ or ‘The Green Ship?’. His own favourite is called ‘Clown’. It’s a story he tells entirely in pictures.

In 1999, Quentin Blake became Britain’s first ever Children’s Laureate. This award lasts for two whole years. I think he deserved it, don’t you?

Some Quentin Blake books - including some from abroad.

Important dates

1932	Quentin Blake was born.
1937	He begins at Lamorbey Primary School.
1943	He goes to Chislehurst and Sidcup Grammar School
1939-45	The Second World War. Quentin is evacuated (sent to live in the country where it was safe) twice during this time.
1949	He sells his first drawing to 'Punch'.
1951-53	National Service.
1953-56	He goes to Cambridge University.
1956-57	He trains to be an English teacher at London University.
1960	With John Yeoman, he publishes 'A Drink of Water'. This is his first children's book.
1965	He begins teaching at the Royal College of Art.
1978	He becomes Head of Illustration at the RCA.
1980	'Mister Magnolia' wins the Kate Greenaway Medal.
1981-89	Quentin's books win awards and prizes.
1988	Quentin retires from the Royal College of Art.
1995	His own favourite book, 'Clown', is published.
1999	Quentin becomes Children's Laureate

Keywords

Children's Laureate
A new award, begun in 1999. It is given to a top writer, poet or illustrator for two years.

Guinea
Twenty-one shillings in old money. Worth about £10 today.

Kate Greenaway Medal
A top prize for children's book illustration.

Light-box
A glass-topped box with a light inside for looking at photos and drawings.

Index